HIYAAA GUYS !!

THANK YOU SO MUCH
FOR BUYING THIS
I HOPE YOU WILL
ENJOY THIS !! ♡♡

LOVE YA!
@KEINOLARAS

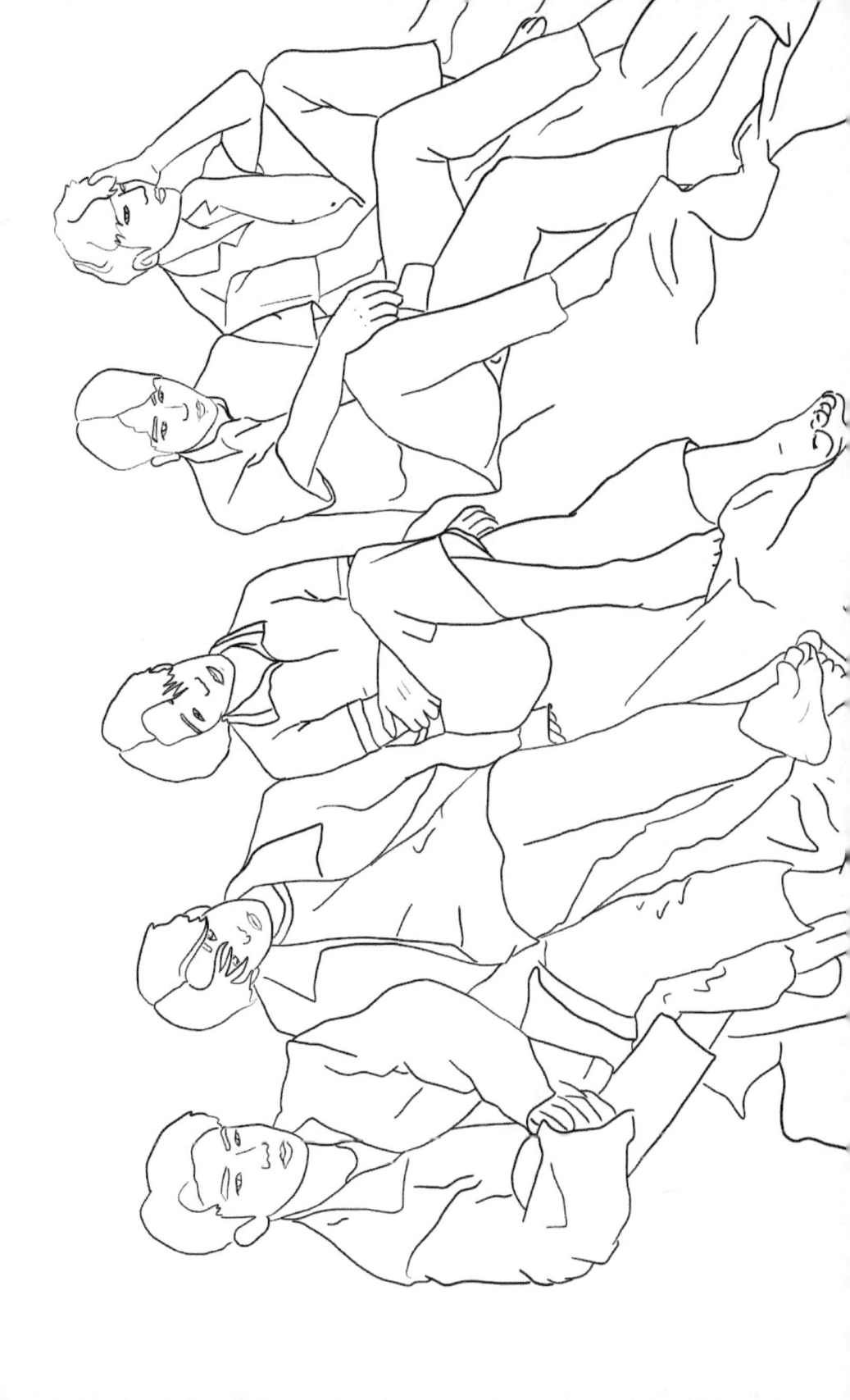

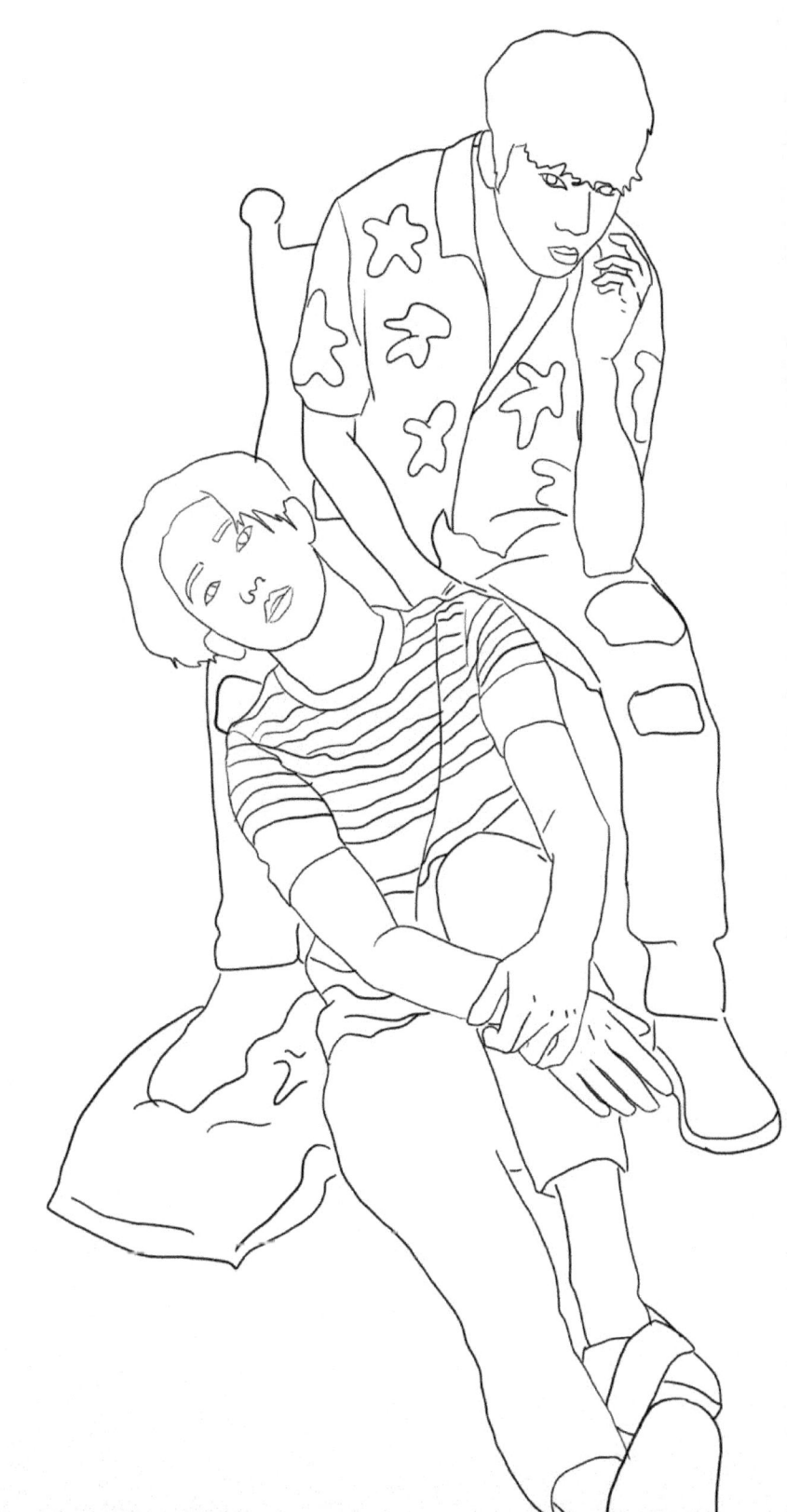

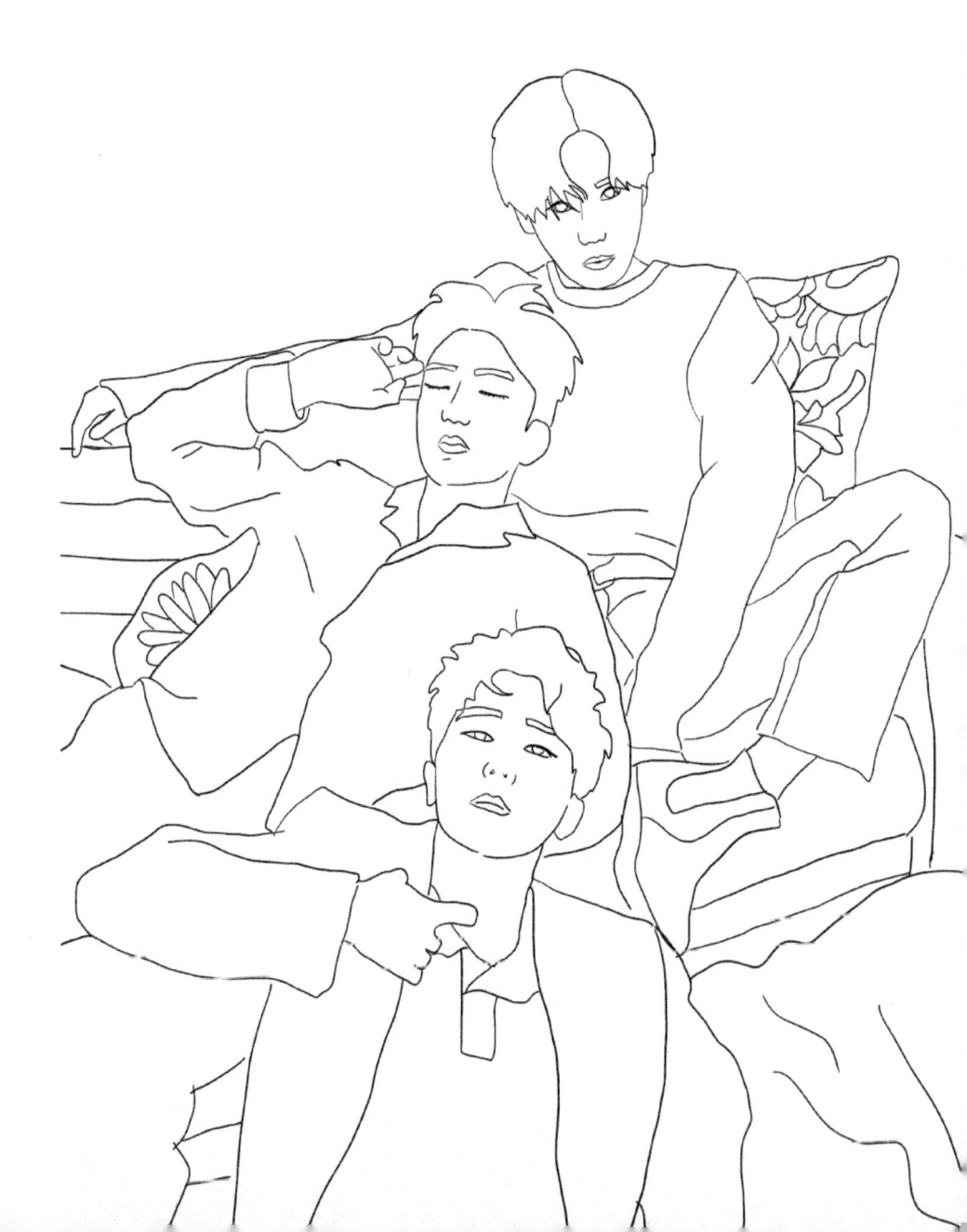

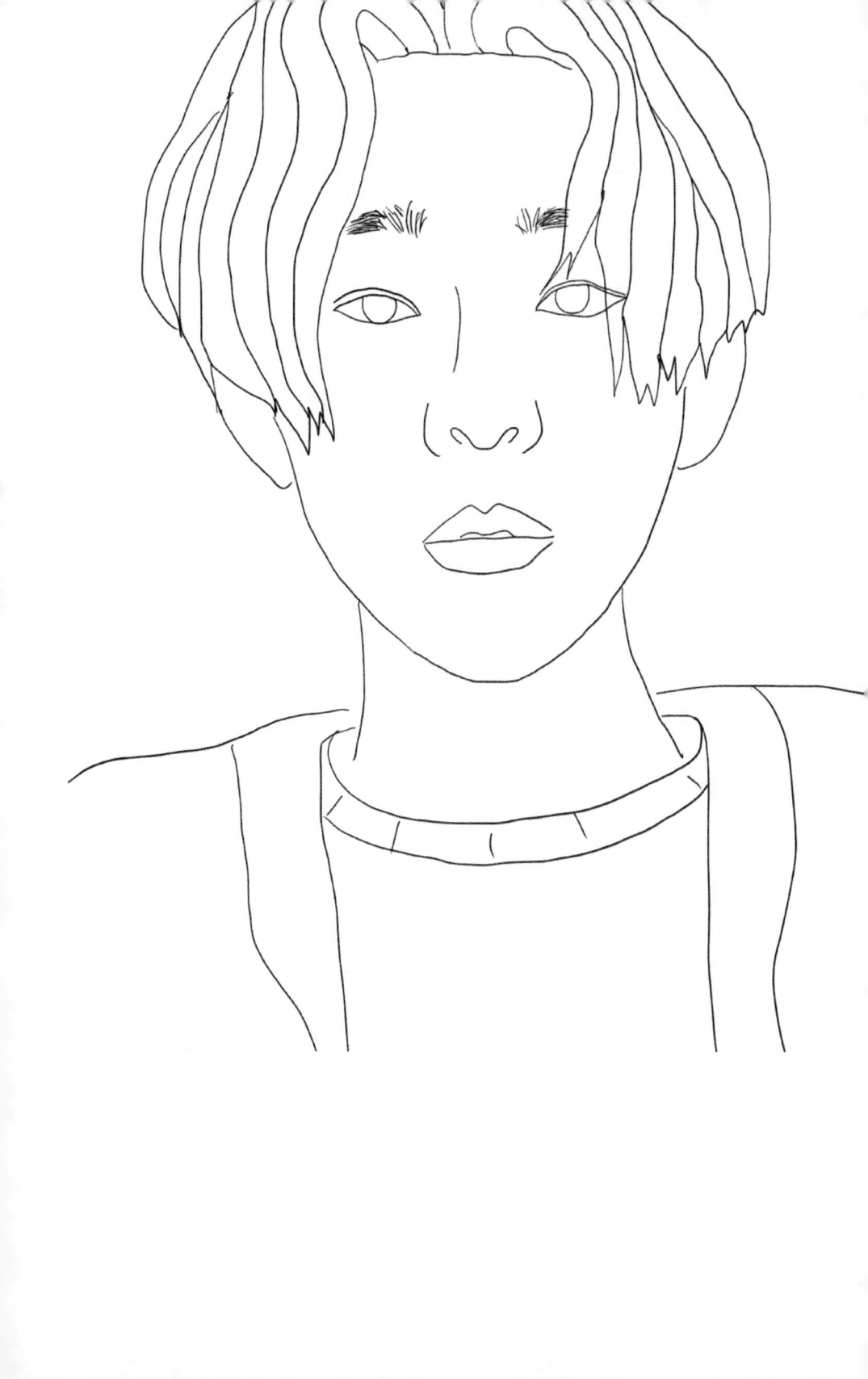

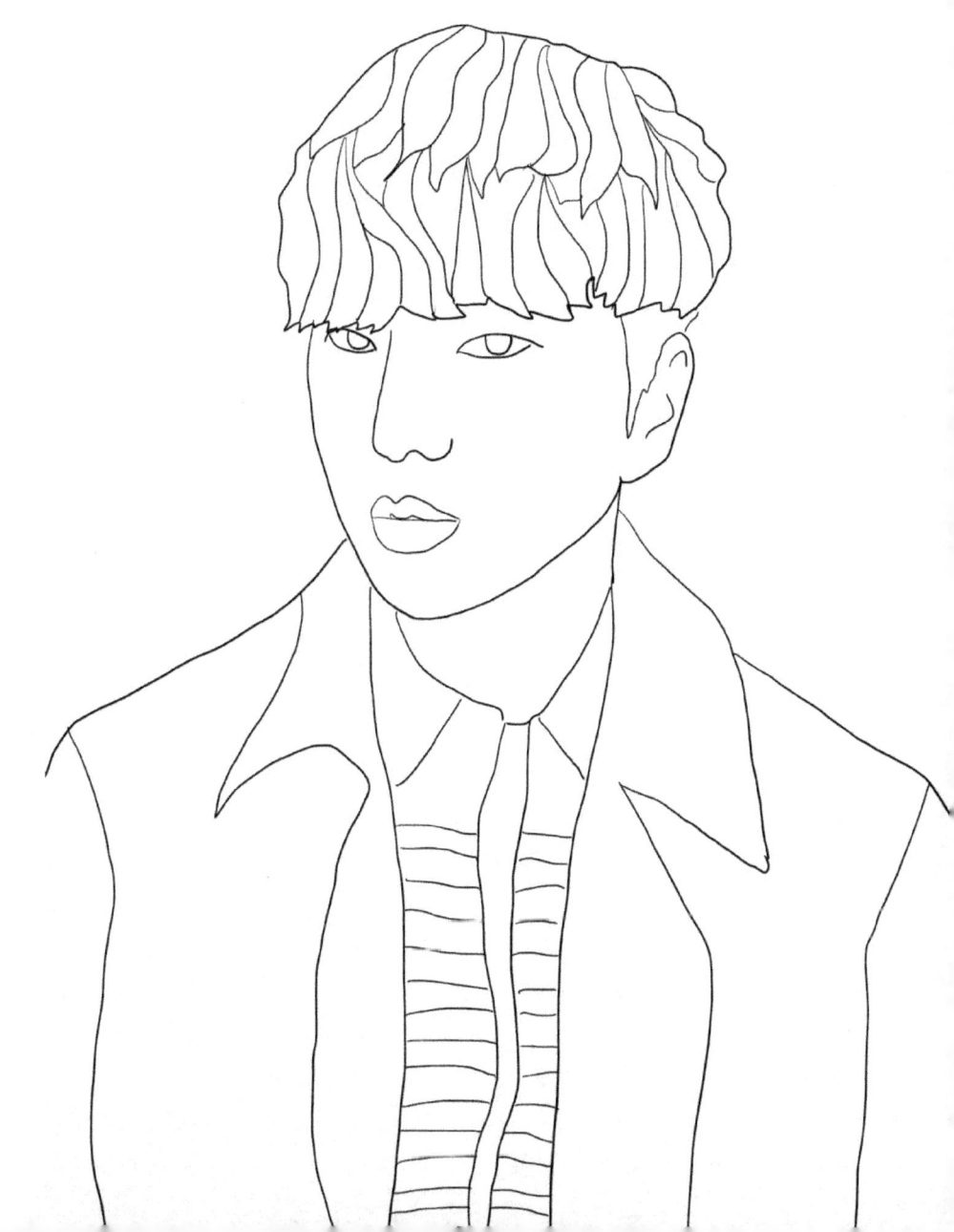

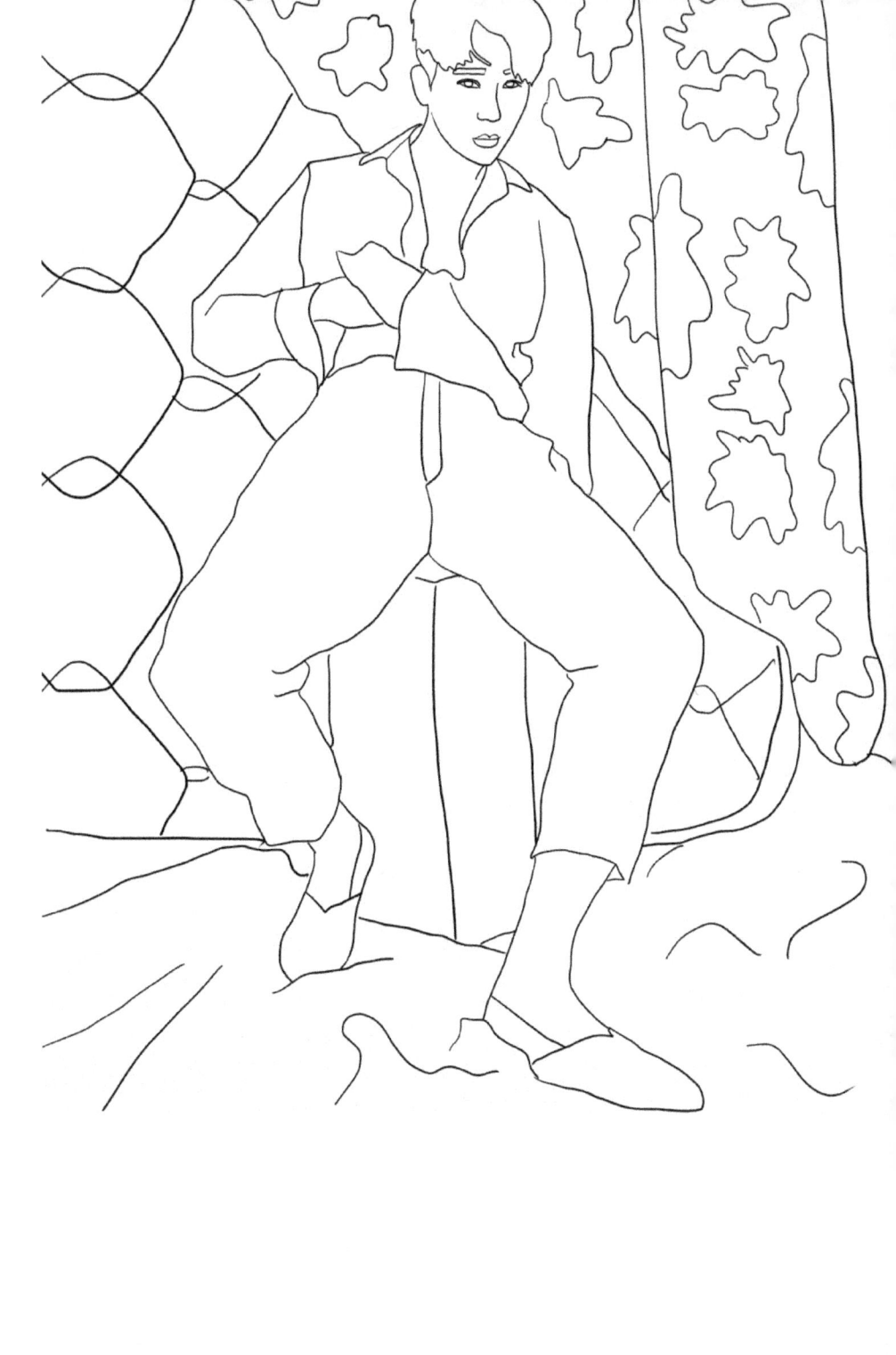

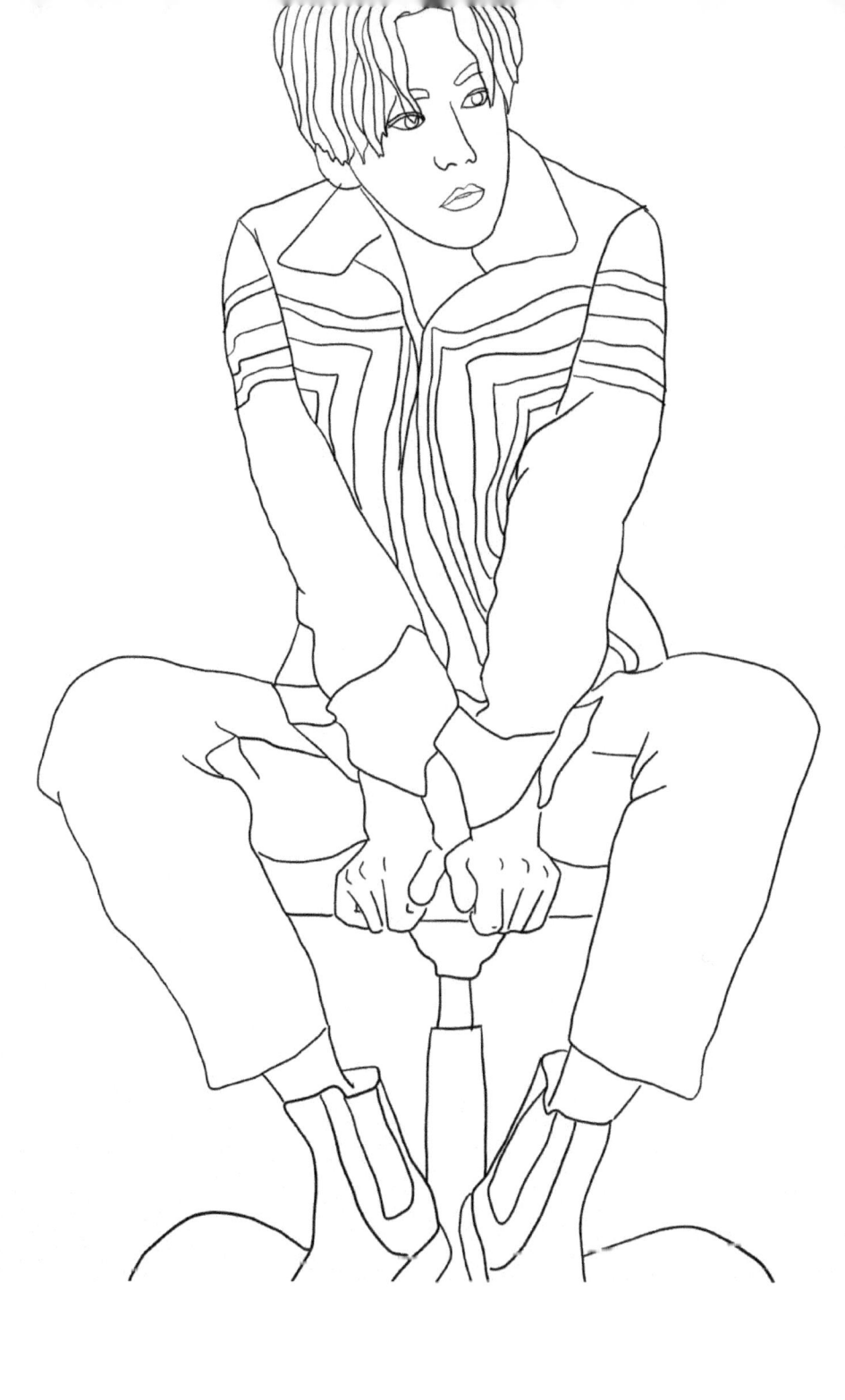

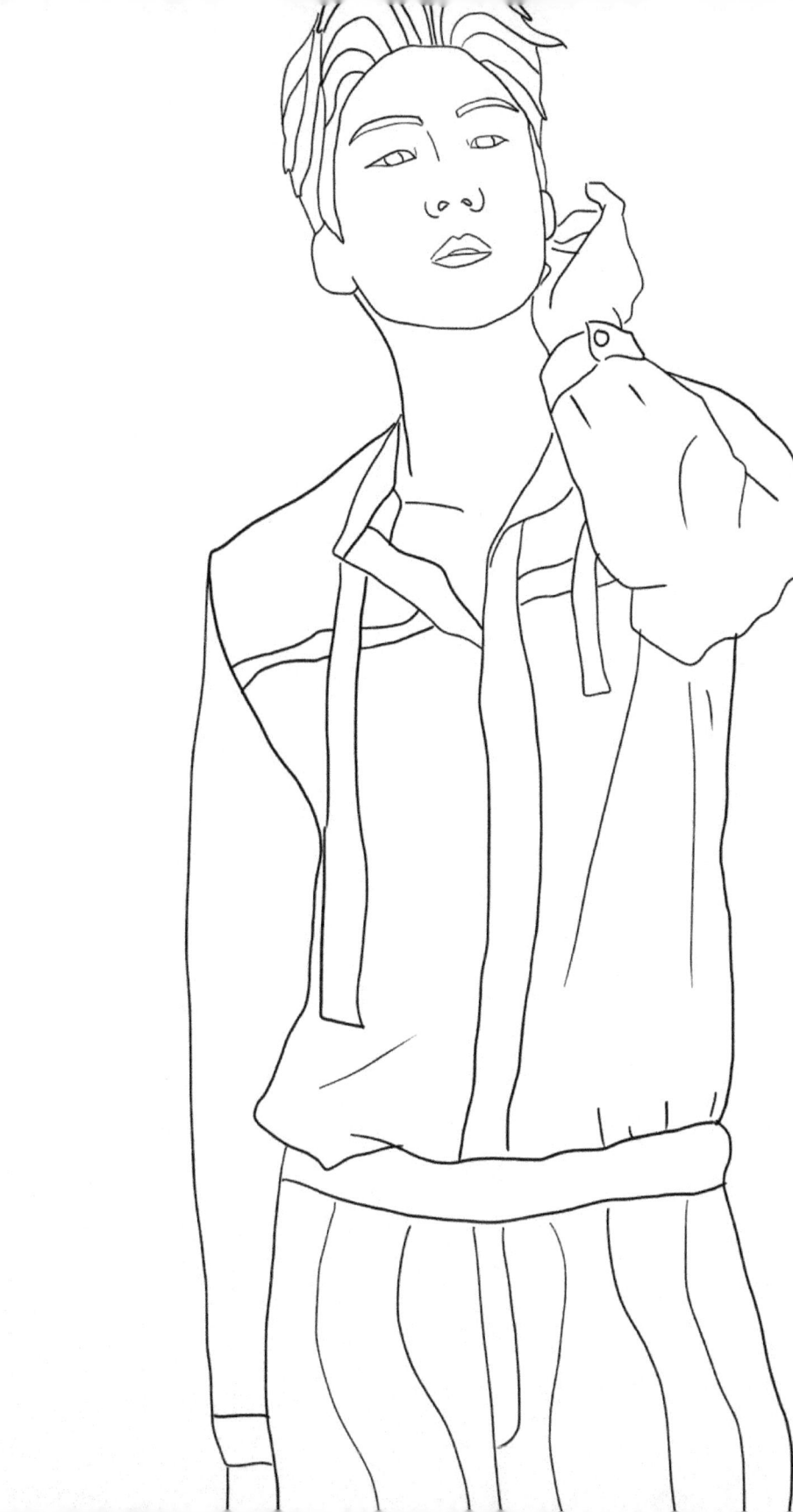

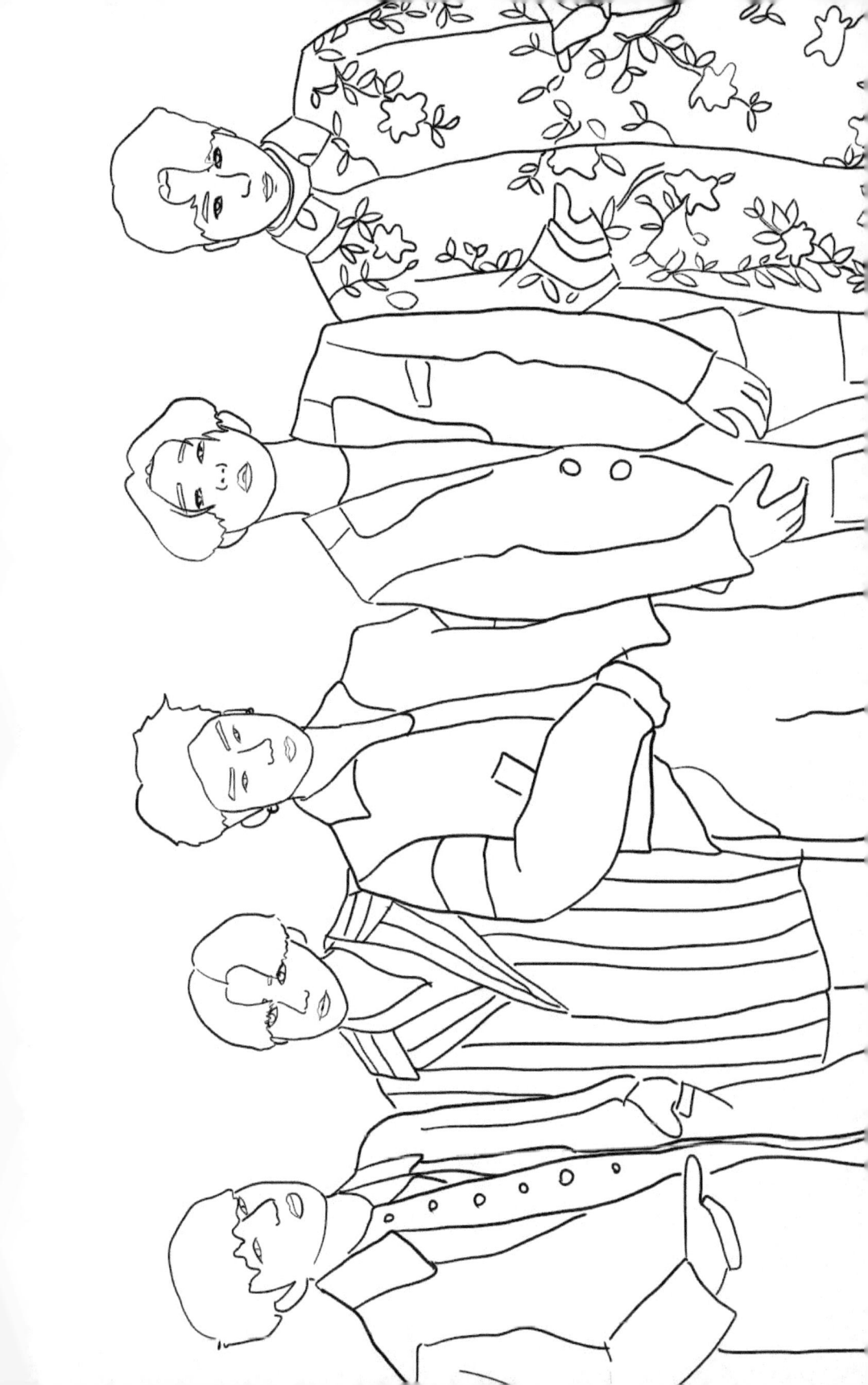

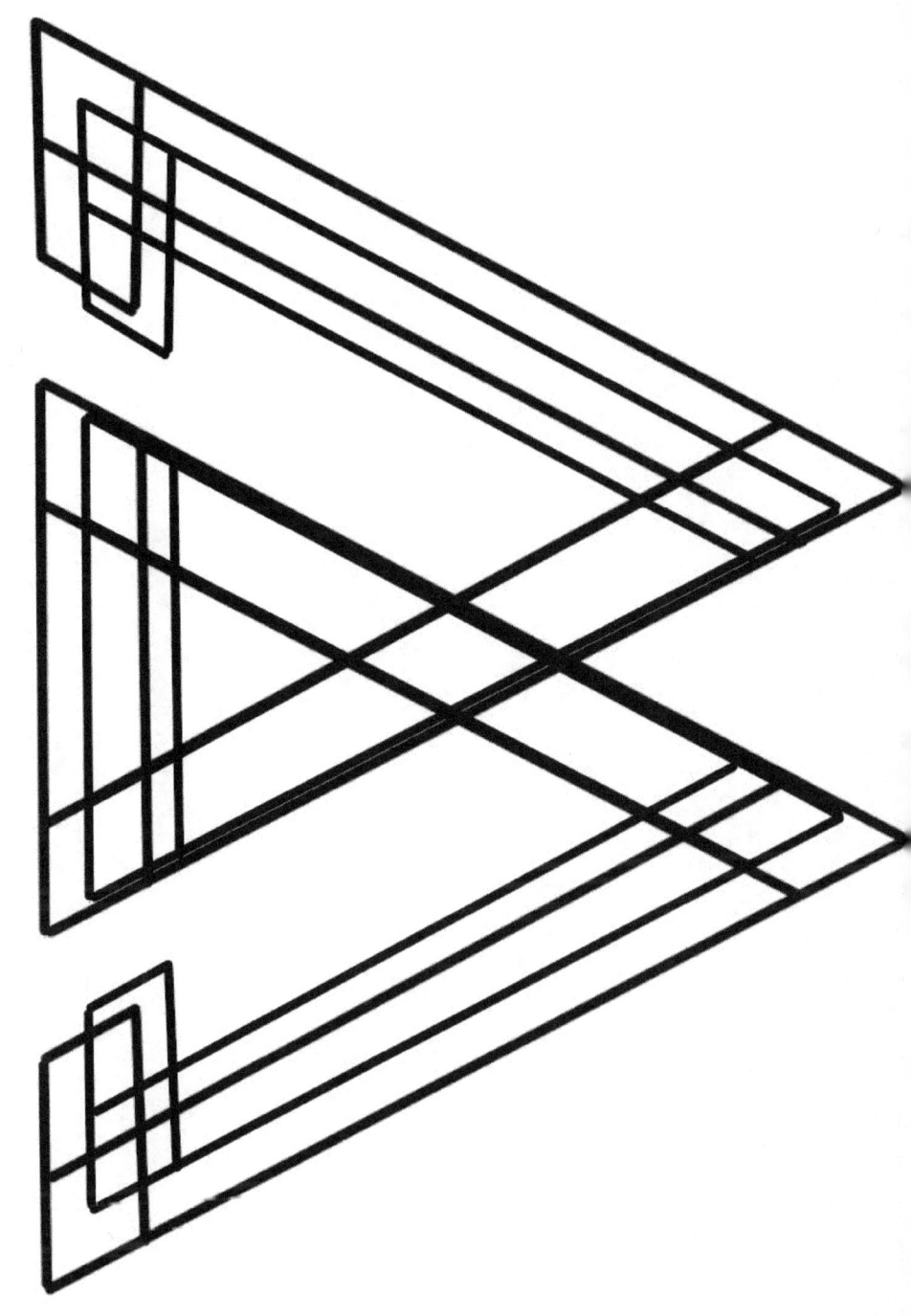

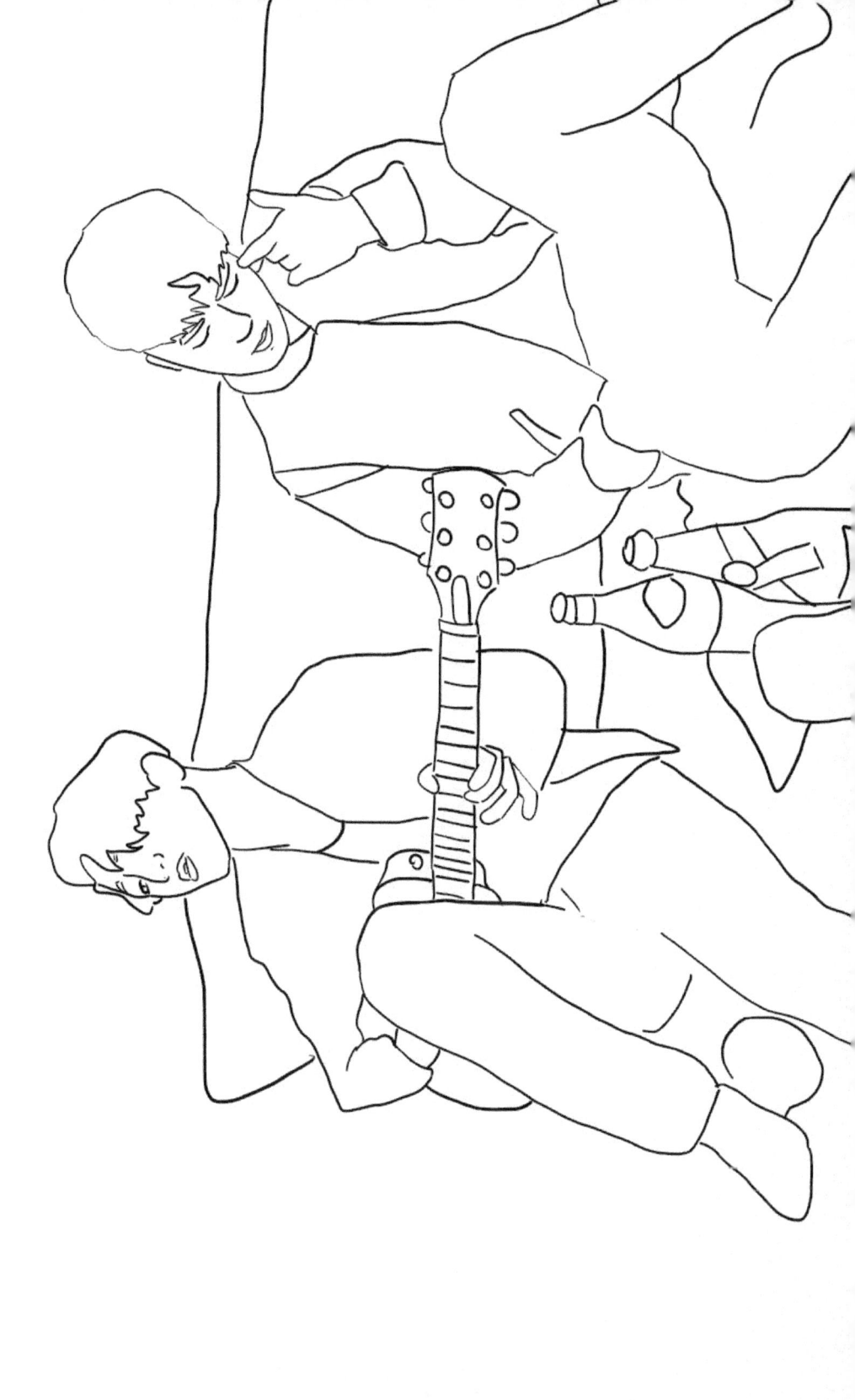

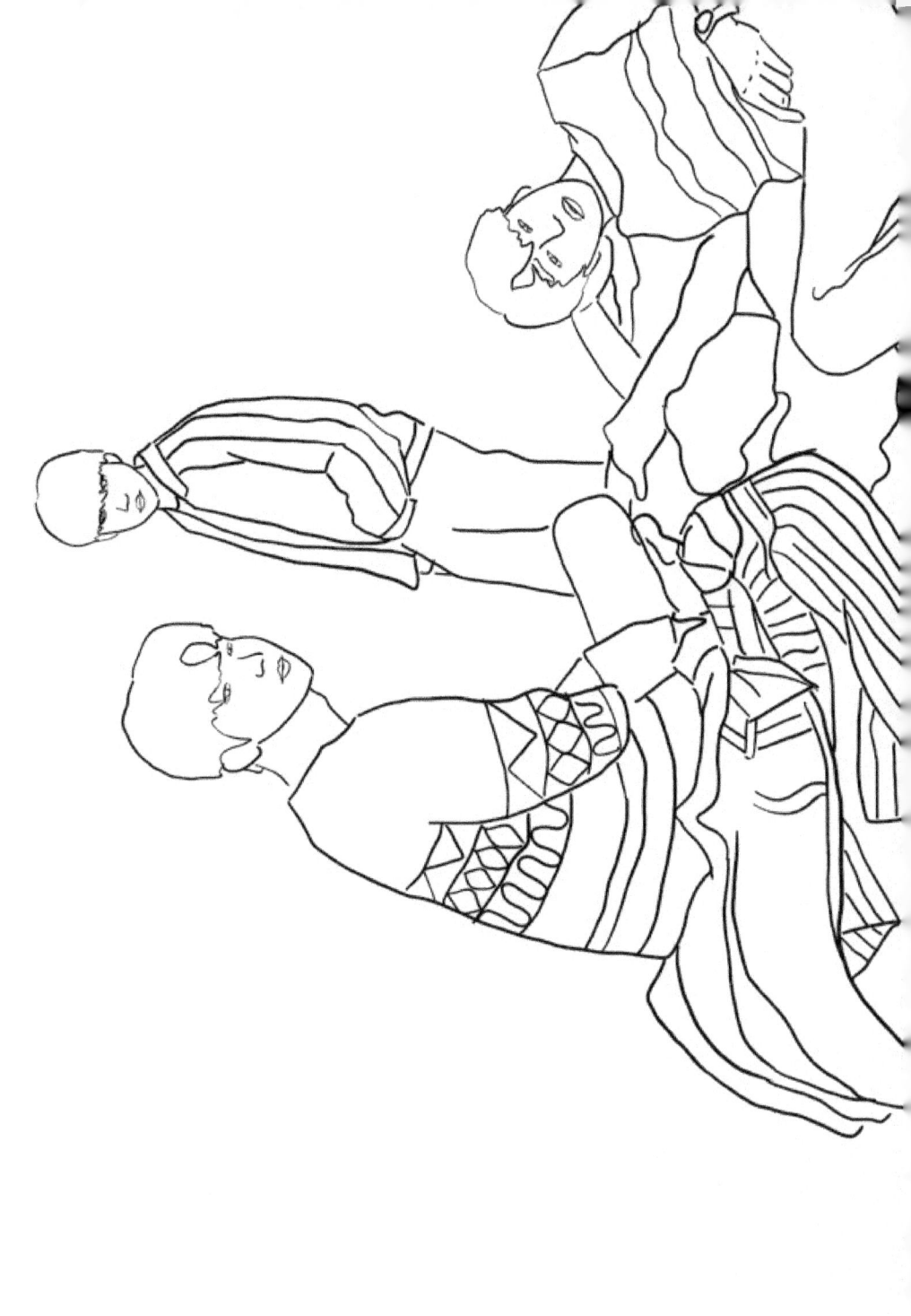

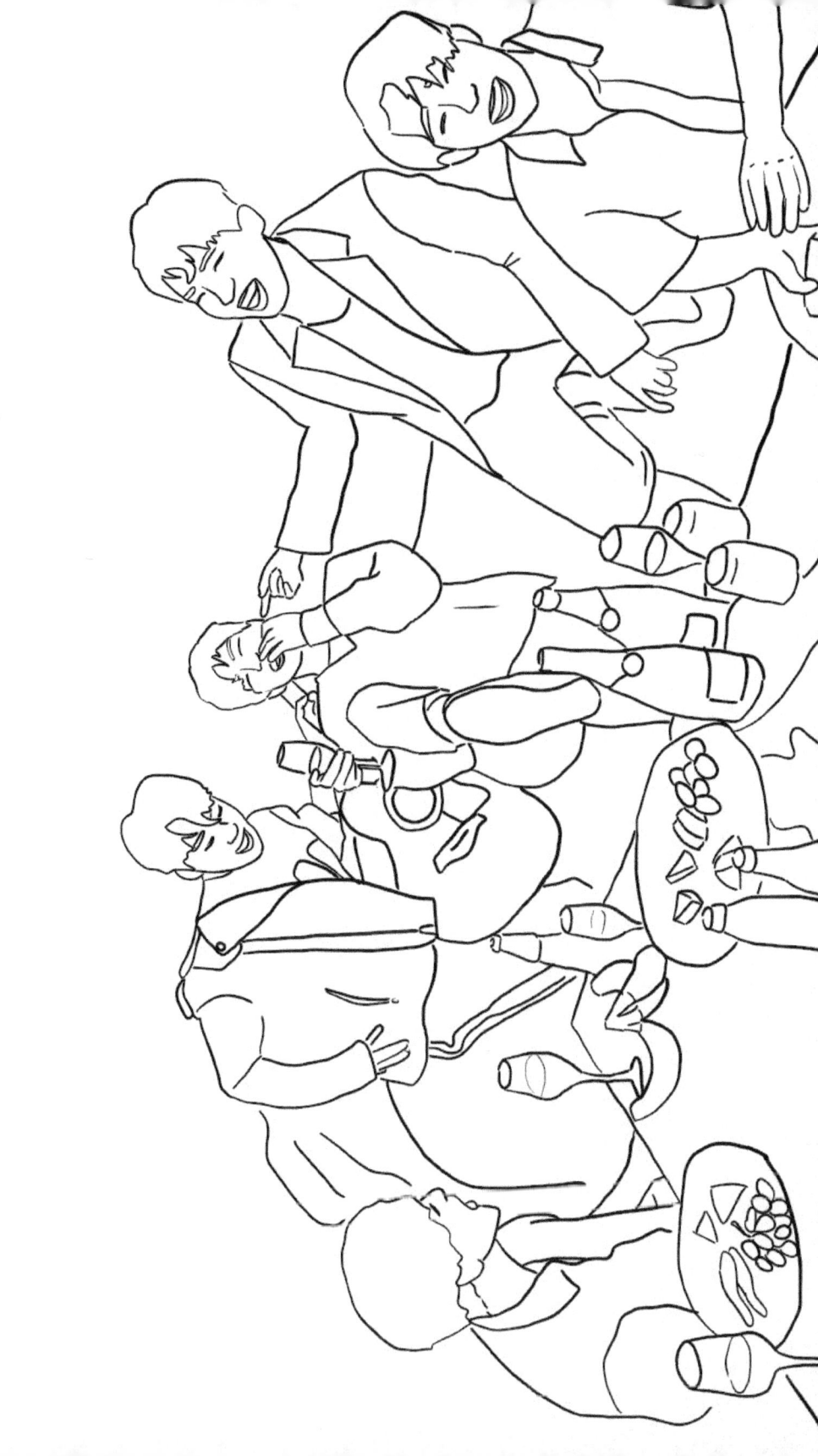

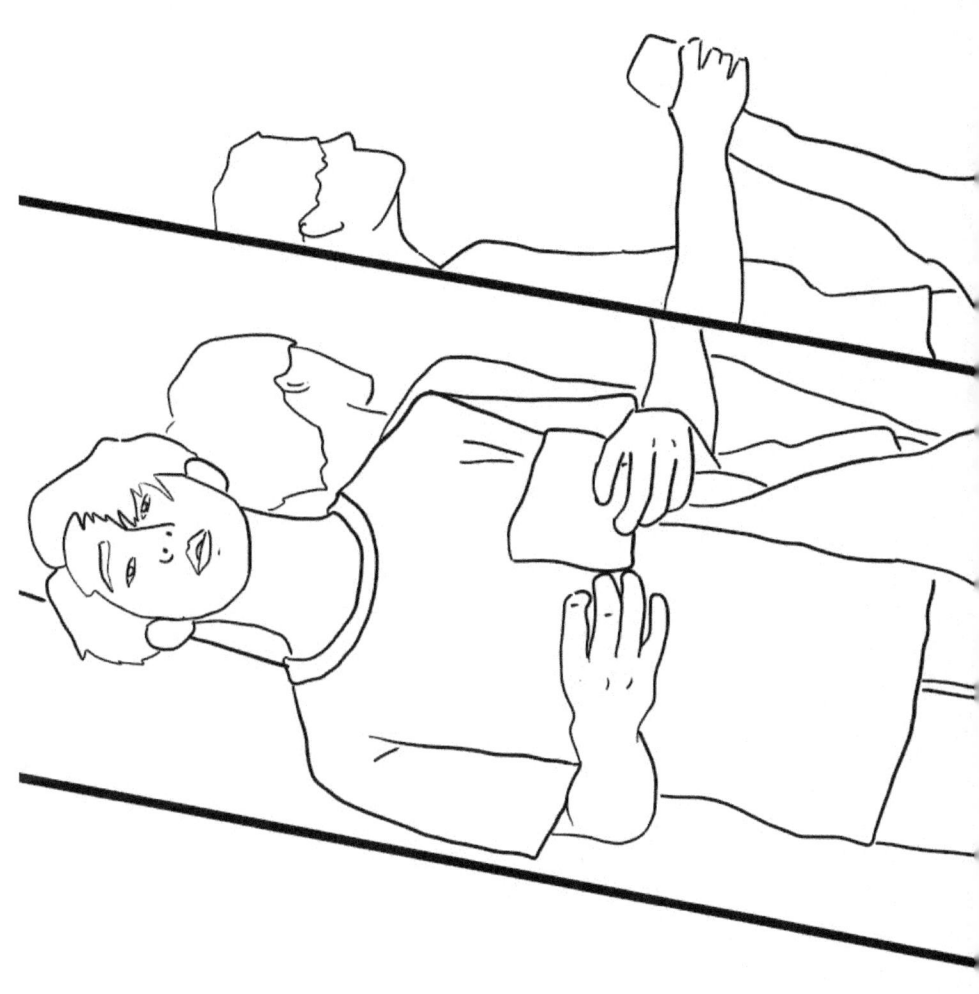

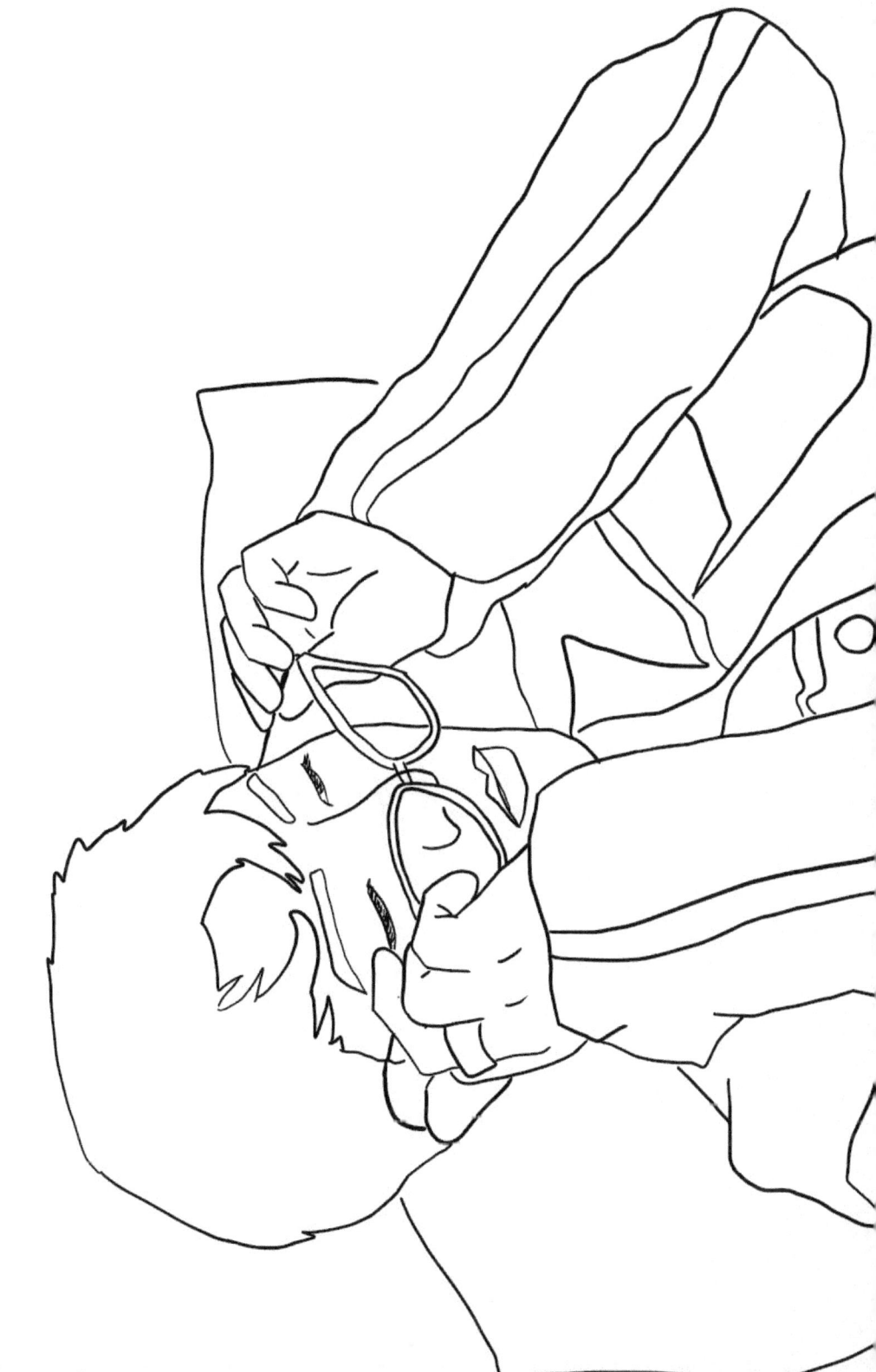

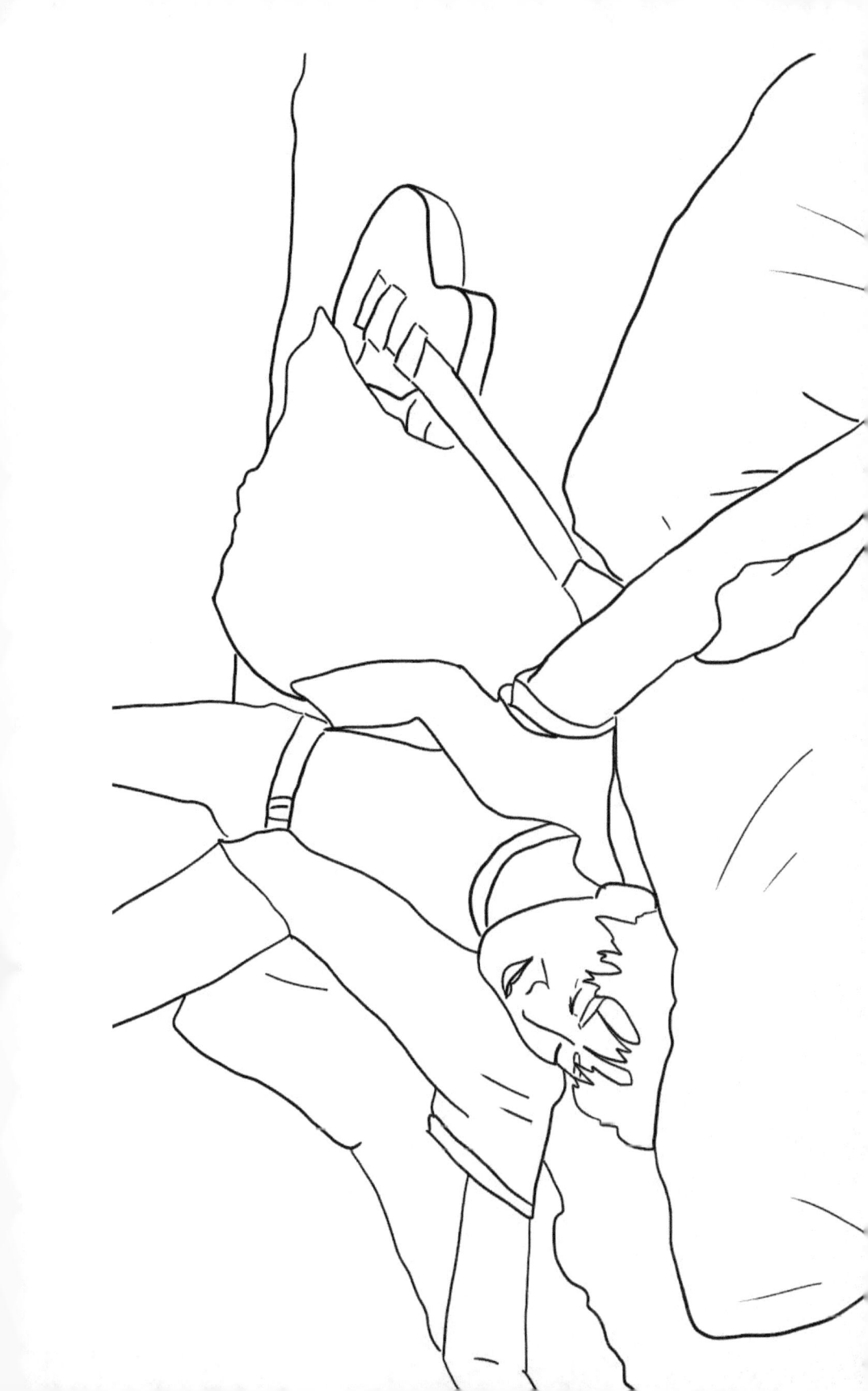

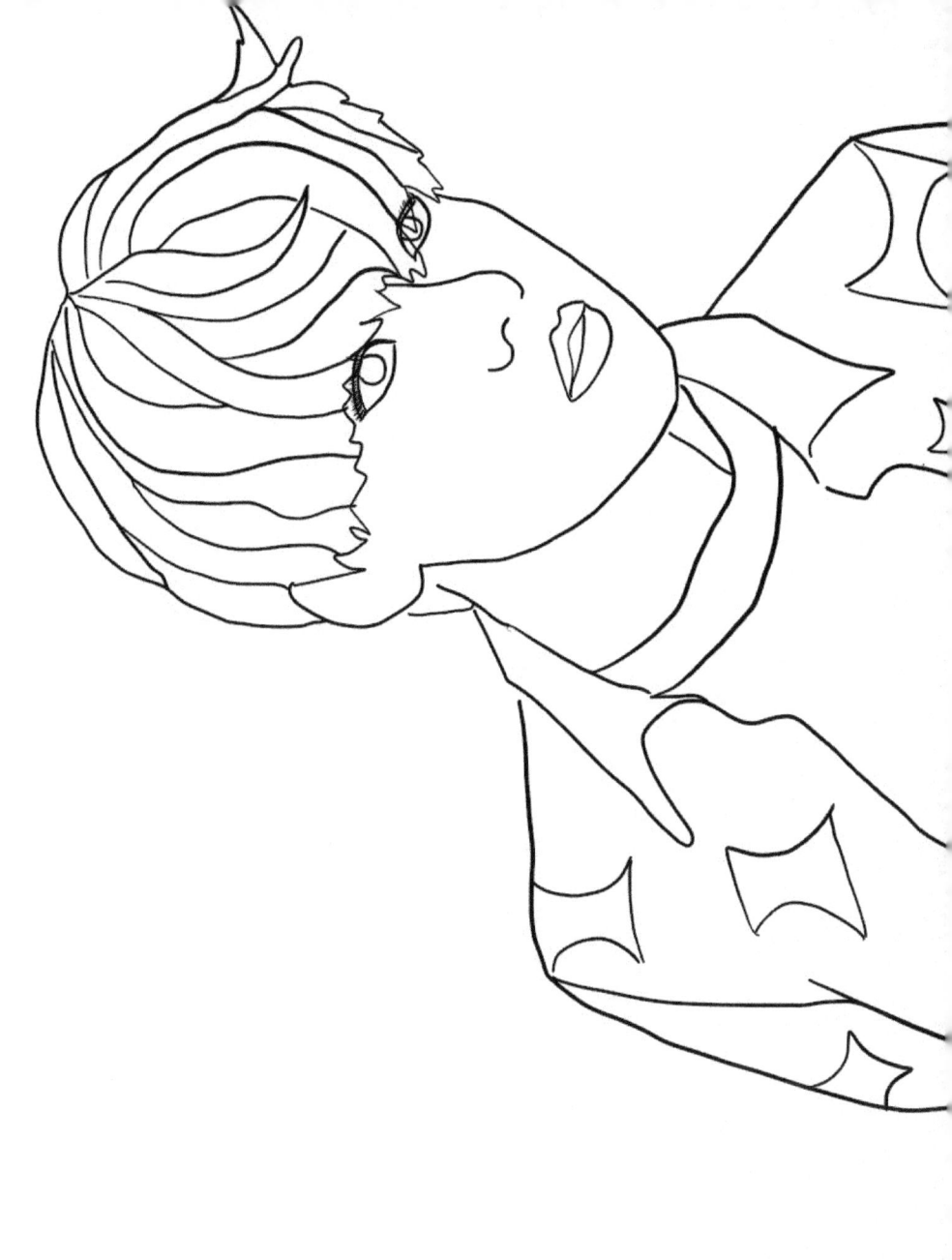

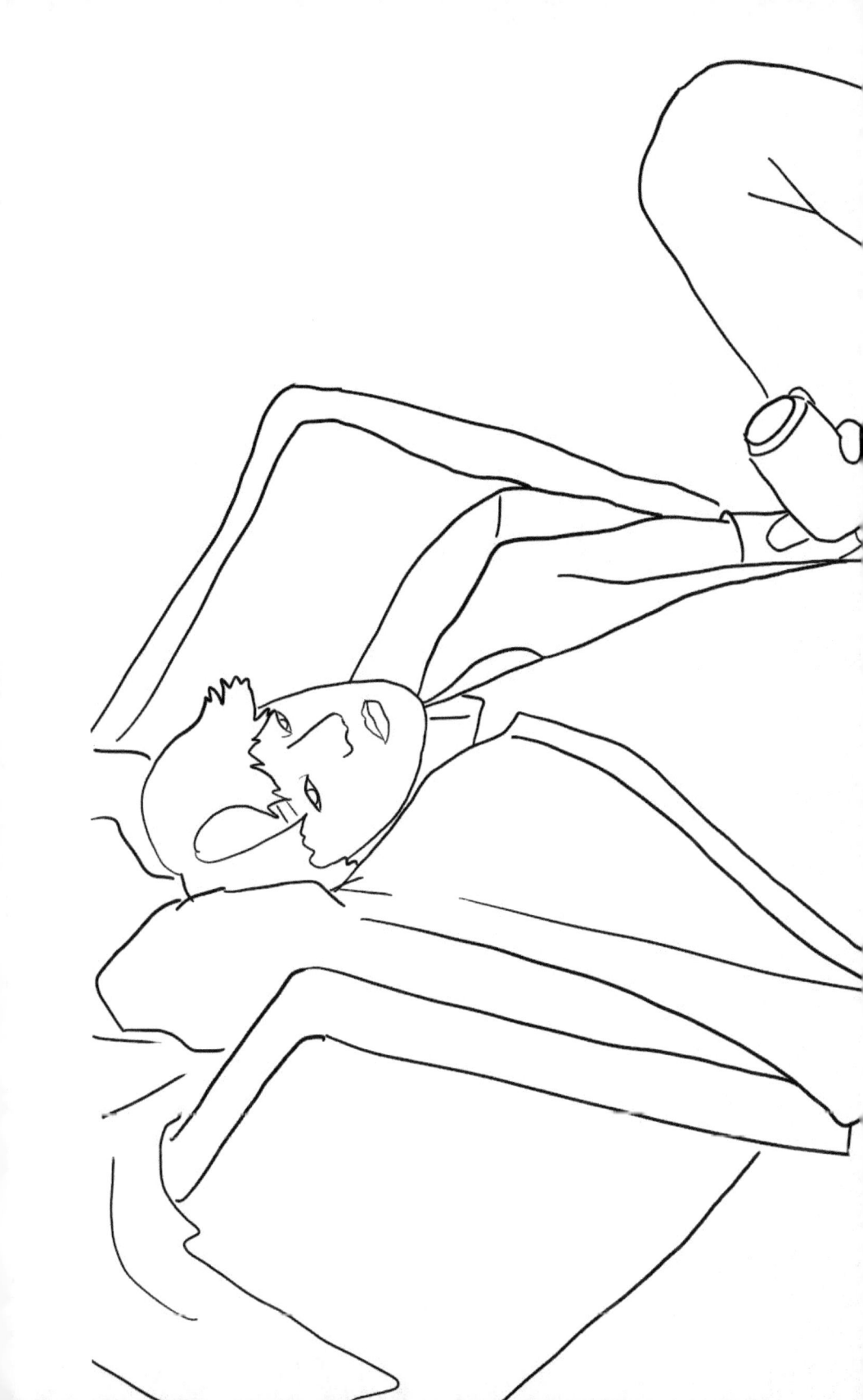

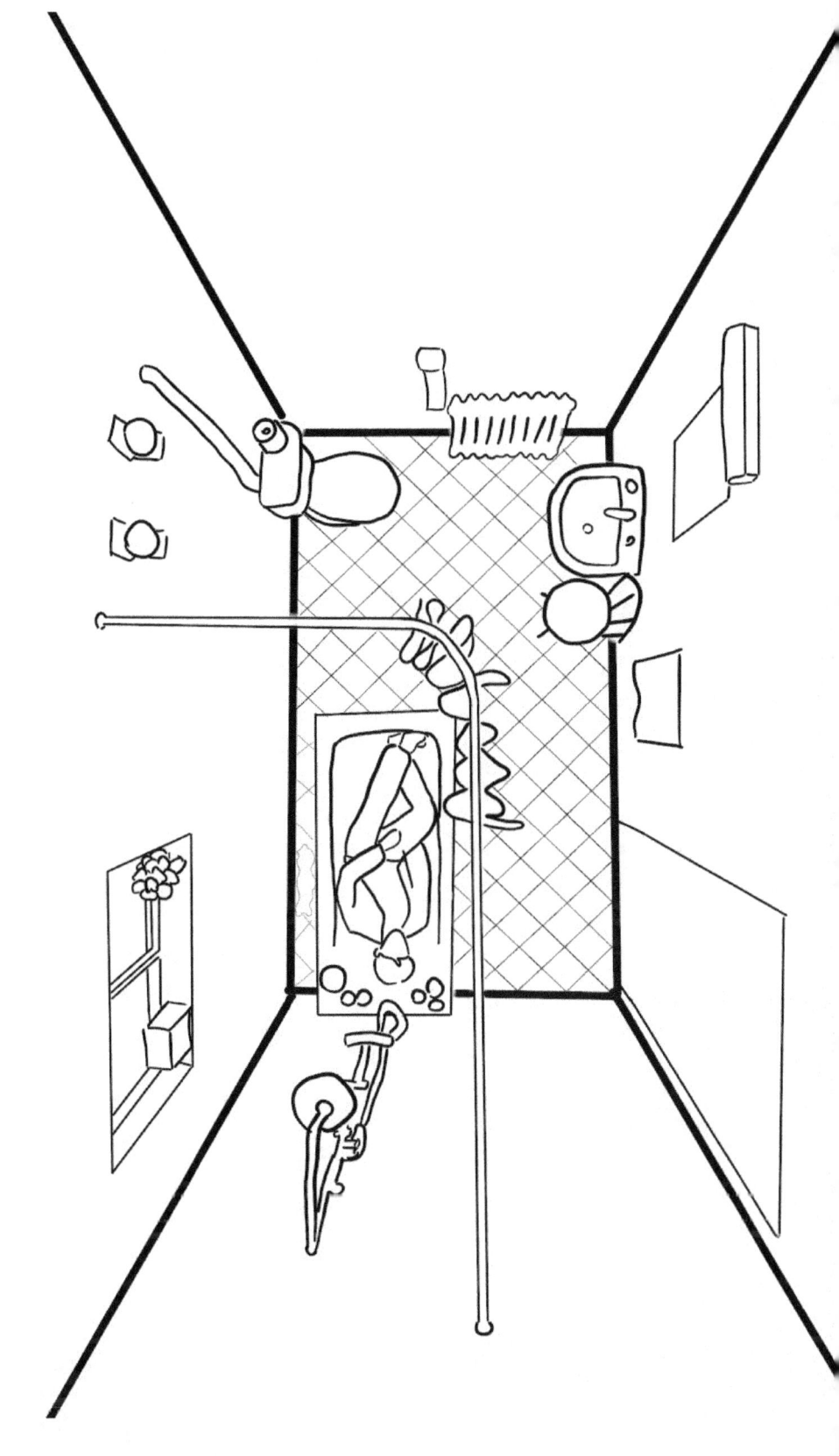

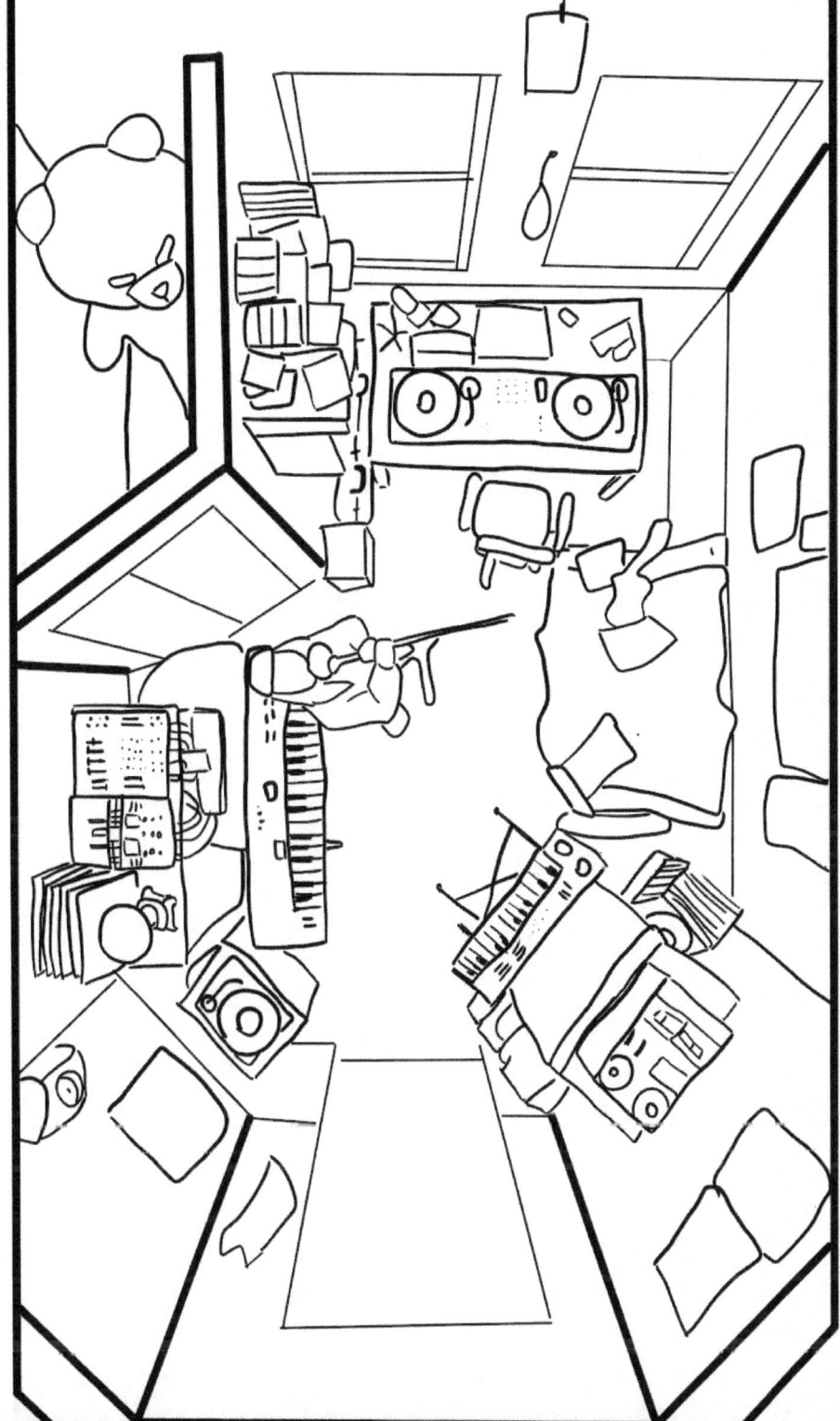

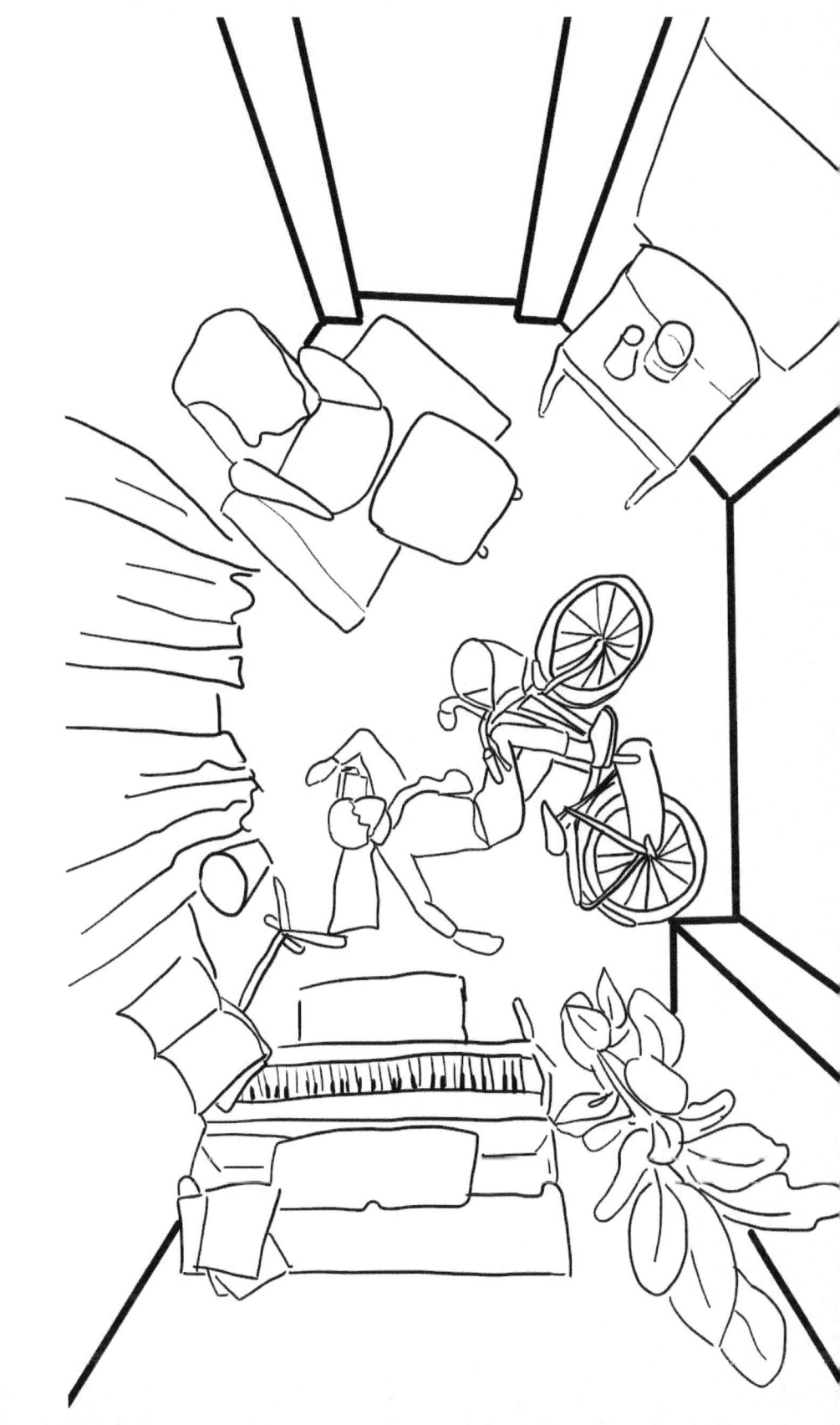

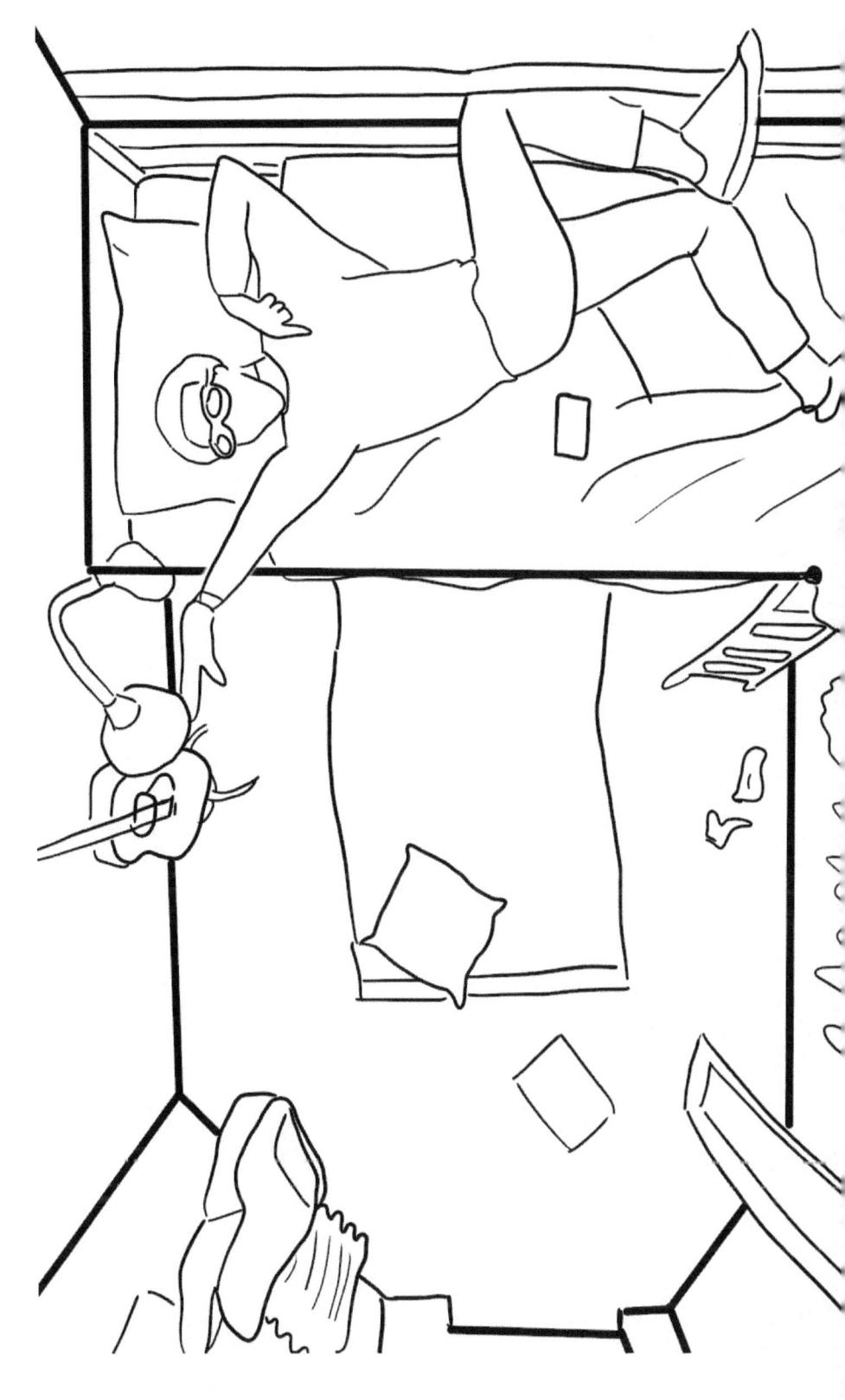

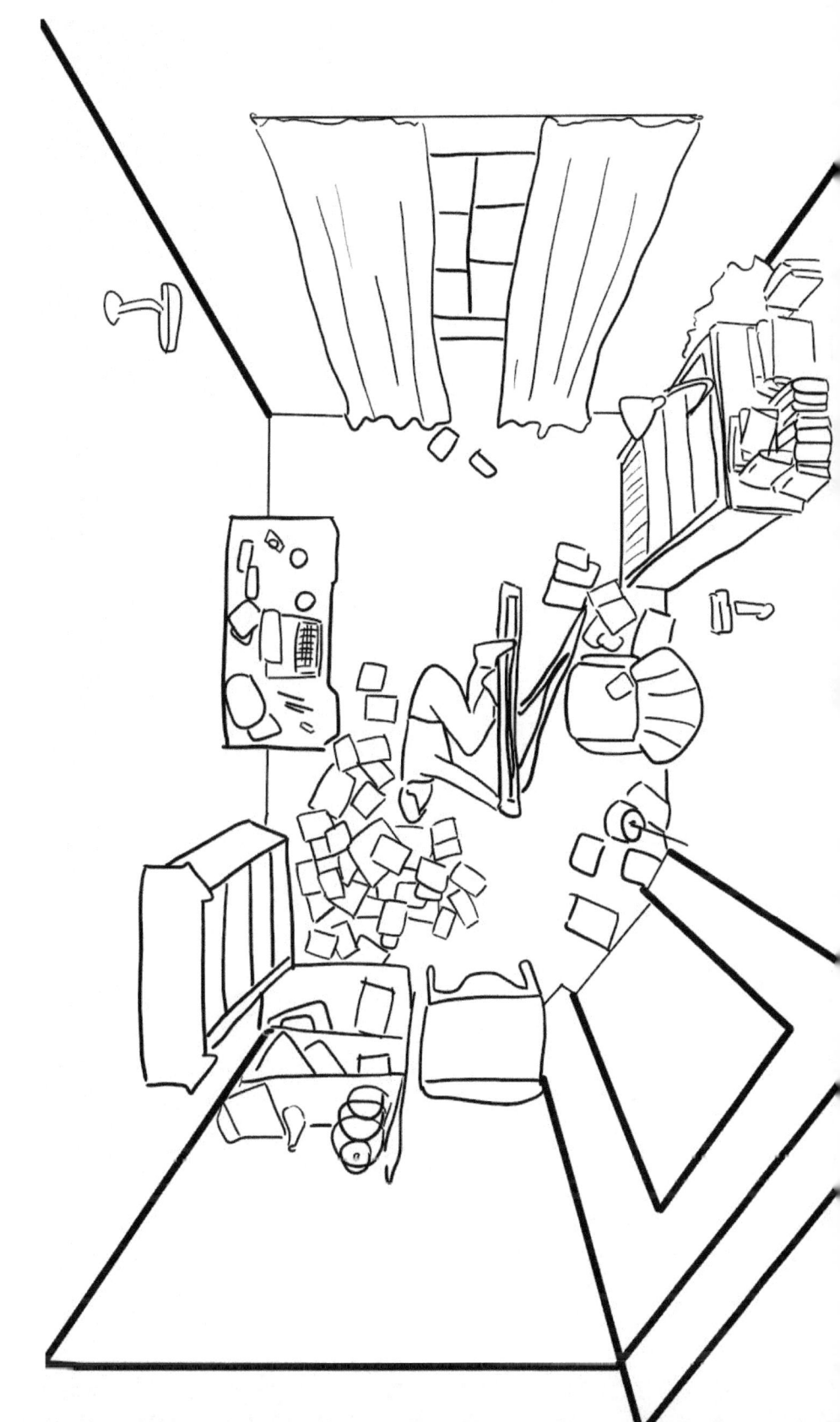

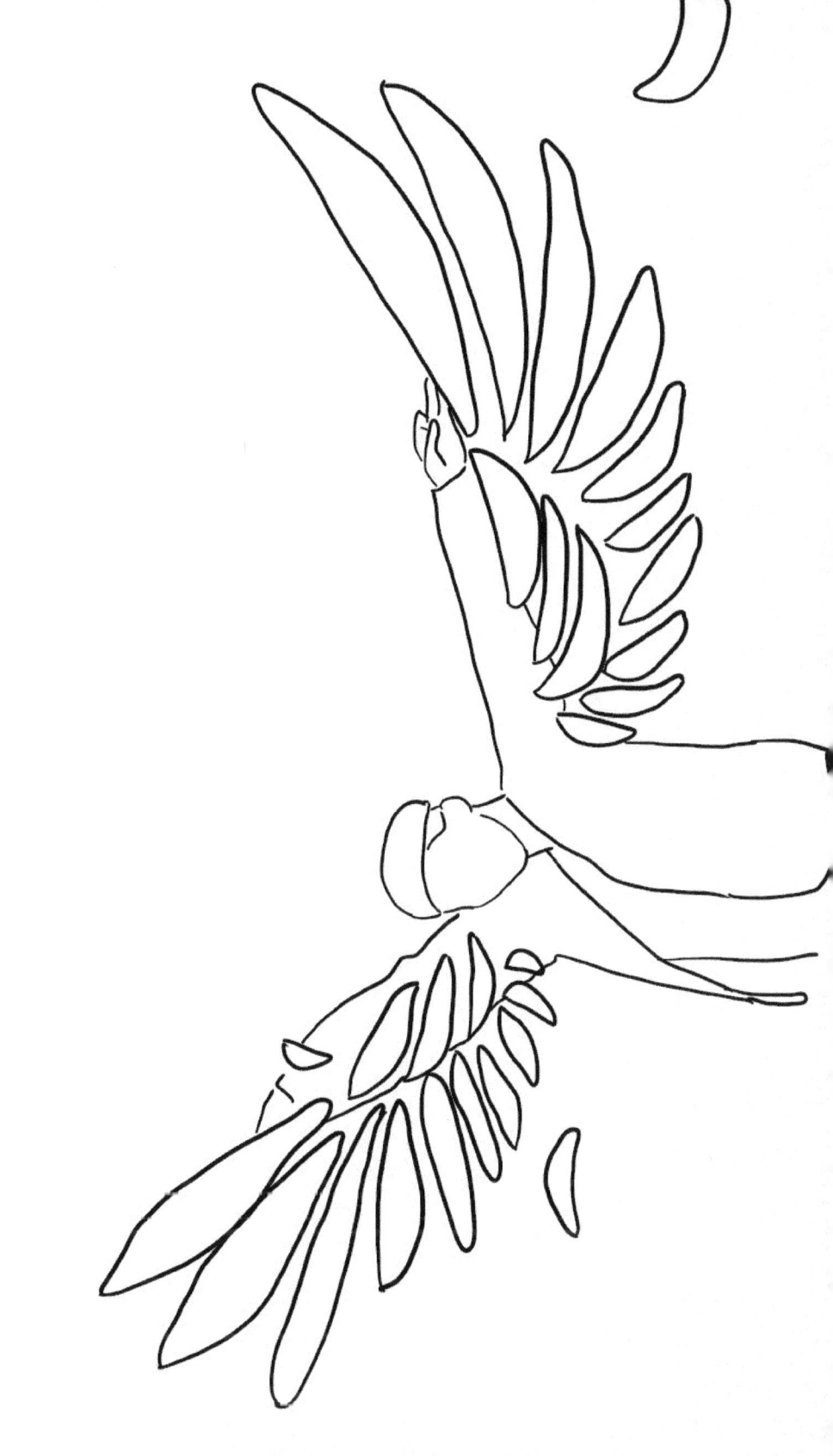

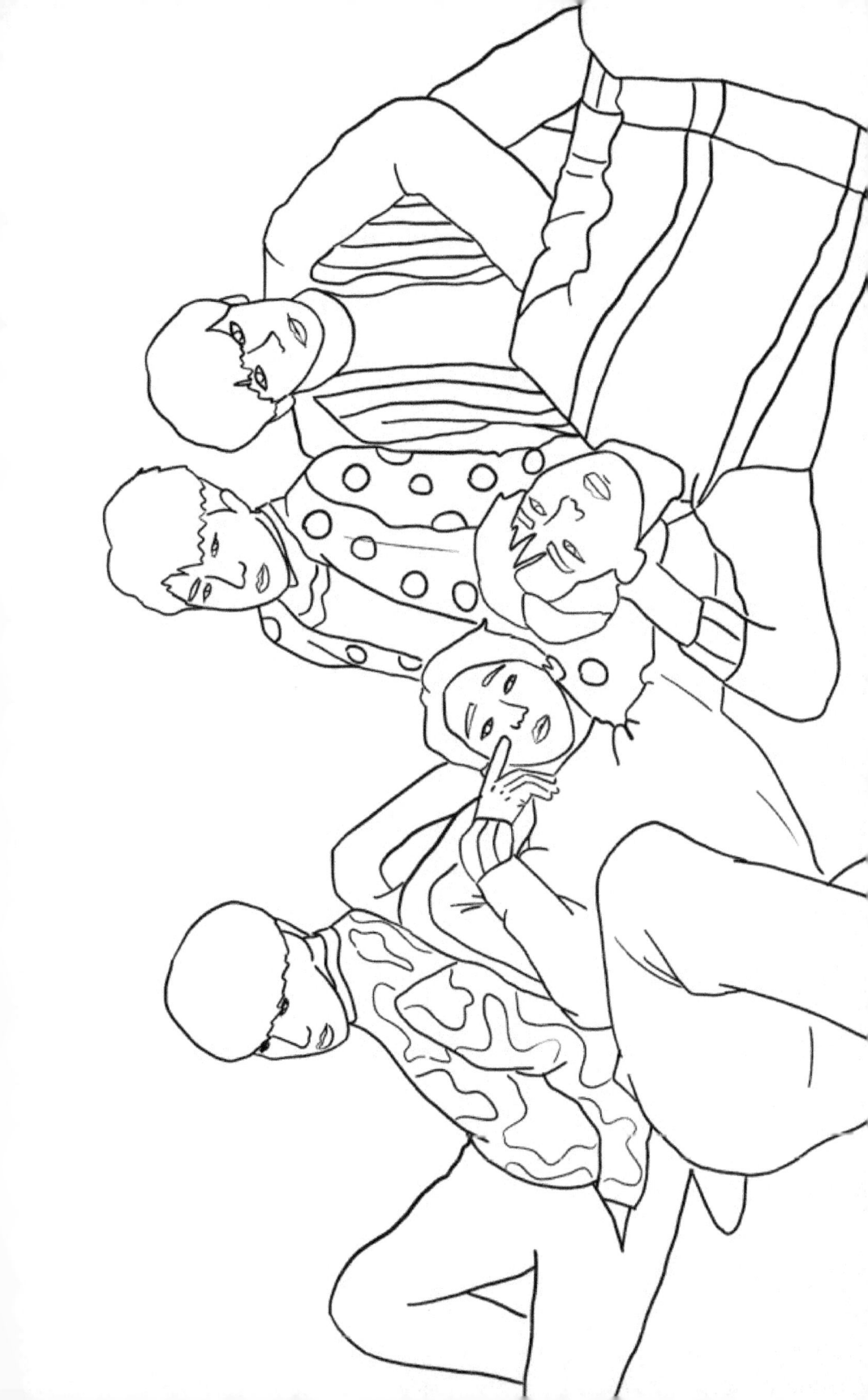

www.ingramcontent.com/pod-product-compliance
Lightning Source LLC
Chambersburg PA
CBHW051822170526
45167CB00005B/2119